The Star-Spangled Banner

CRAB ORCHARD AWARD SERIES IN POETRY

The Star-Spangled

★

★

Banner

Denise Duhamel

Crab Orchard Review

&

Southern Illinois University Press

Carbondale and Edwardsville

Printed in the United States of America

02   01   00   99   4   3   2   1

The Crab Orchard Award Series in Poetry is a joint publishing
venture of Southern Illinois University Press and *Crab Orchard Review.*
This series has been made possible by the generous support of the Office
of the President of Southern Illinois University and the Office of the
Vice Chancellor for Academic Affairs and Provost at Southern Illinois
University at Carbondale.

Library of Congress Cataloging-in-Publication Data
Duhamel, Denise.
The Star-Spangled Banner / Denise Duhamel
p.   cm. — (Crab Orchard award series in poetry)
I. Title.   II. Series.
PS3554.U3968S73   1999
811'.54—dc21   98-50622
ISBN 0-8093-2259-5 (pbk. : alk. paper)   CIP

The paper used in this publication meets the minimum requirements of
American National Standard for Information Sciences—Permanence of
Paper for Printed Library Materials, ANSI Z39.48-1984. ∞

Crab Orchard Award Series in Poetry Editor: Jon Tribble
Judge for 1998: Rodney Jones

For Nick

Contents

~

Acknowledgments

The author gratefully acknowledges the magazines and anthologies where these poems first appeared:

Asian Pacific American Journal—"*Bangungot*"

Charlotte Poetry Review—"Art"

Chiron Review—"Skipping Breakfast" (under the title "How I Barely Have Time to Write This Poem and the Worst Thing about Work Is Having to Wear Shoes All Day")

Cincinnati Poetry Review—"White Virgin"

Controlled Burn—"Nick at Nite" (under the title "Swing American")

Crab Orchard Review—"Yes"

5 AM—"Grace"

Gargoyle—"Lines"

Global City Review—"Fairy Tale," "Scared about What Was There" (under the title "Animals and the Zoo"), "I'm Dealing with My Pain"

Harrisburg Review—"Where to Find Feminine Protection While Traveling in a Foreign Country"

Indiana Review—"*Insomnio*," "The Therapist's Funeral" (under the title "The Jet Lag of the Newly Dead")

Long Shot—"The Little I Know about Eyes"

Magma (England)—"Another Poem Called 'Sphincter'"

Ontario Review—"Stranger," "Cockroaches," "Surgery," "June 13, 1995"

phati'tude—"The Star-Spangled Banner"

Poetry New York—"Sex with a Famous Poet"

Salt Hill Review—"The Difference Between Pepsi and Pope," "Happy Ending"

Sheila-Na-Gig—"How Much Is This Poem Going to Cost Me?" "Husband as a Second Language"

Third Coast—"A Kissing," *"Playa Naturista"*

Urbanus—"House-Sitting"

Willow Springs—"Tulip"

Zone 3—"Noctilucae"

"The Difference Between Pepsi and Pope" appears in *The Best American Poetry 1998*. That same poem is also reprinted, along with "Happy Ending," in *Poetry Nation*.

Thanks, too, to those who read the manuscript in progress: Regie Cabico, Tom Fink, Jenny Pierson, Maureen Seaton, and especially Stephanie Strickland. And to those who helped edit it post-acceptance: Rodney Jones and Jon Tribble. And for the gift of time, thanks to The Corporation of Yaddo, Funcacíon Valparaíso, and The Ludwig Vogelstein Foundation.

Yes

According to *Culture Shock:*
A Guide to Customs and Etiquette
of Filipinos, when my husband says yes,
he could also mean one of the following:
a.) *I don't know.*
b.) *If you say so.*
c.) *If it will please you.*
d.) *I hope I have said yes unenthusiastically enough*
for you to realize I mean no.
You can imagine the confusion
surrounding our movie dates, the laundry,
who will take out the garbage
and when. I remind him
I'm an American, that all his yeses sound alike to me.
I tell him here in America we have shrinks
who can help him to be less of a people-pleaser.
We have two-year-olds who love to scream "No!"
when they don't get their way. I tell him,
in America we have a popular book,
When I Say No I Feel Guilty.
"Should I get you a copy?" I ask.
He says yes, but I think he means
"If it will please you," i.e., "I won't read it."
"I'm trying," I tell him, "but you have to try too."
"Yes," he says, then makes *tampo,*
a sulking that the book *Culture Shock* describes as
"subliminal hostility . . . withdrawal of customary cheerfulness
in the presence of the one who has displeased" him.
The book says it's up to me to make things all right,
"to restore goodwill, not by talking the problem out,
but by showing concern about the wounded person's
well-being." Forget it, I think, even though I know
if I'm not nice, *tampo* can quickly escalate into *nagdadabog*—
foot stomping, grumbling, the slamming
of doors. Instead of talking to my husband, I storm off

to talk to my porcelain Kwan Yin,
the Chinese goddess of mercy
that I bought on Canal Street years before
my husband and I started dating.
"The real Kwan Yin is in Manila,"
he tells me. "She's called Nuestra Señora de Guia.
Her Asian features prove Christianity
was in the Philippines before the Spanish arrived."
My husband's telling me this
tells me he's sorry. Kwan Yin seems to wink,
congratulating me—my short prayer worked.
"Will you love me forever?" I ask,
then study his lips, wondering if I'll be able to decipher
what he means by his yes.

The Difference Between Pepsi and Pope

I have this blind spot, a dark line, thin as a hair, that obliterates
a stroke of scenery on the right side of my field of vision
so that often I get whole words at the end of sentences wrong
like when I first saw the title of David Lehman's poem
"The Difference Between Pepsi and Coke" and I misread
"Coke" for "Pope." This blind spot makes me a terrible driver,
a bad judge of distances, a ping-pong player that inspires giggles
from the opposite team.
                        I knew a poet who dressed up as a cookie
and passed out a new brand in a crowded supermarket.
The next day he gave the Pepsi Challenge to passersby
in a mall.
                I felt old-fashioned admitting to this poet that I prefer Coke,
that wavy hyphen that separates its full name Coca~Cola.
Like the bar let down in the limbo dance, the Spanish tilde comes down until
not even a lower-case letter can squeeze under it.
I searched for that character recently, writing to David Lehman,
telling him about an electronic magazine, the address of which
had this ~ in it. I couldn't find it, although I stared
at my computer keyboard for more than a few minutes.
I only noticed it today in the upper left hand corner, above the tab,
the alternate of ', if you hit the shift key. I wonder if I also have a blind spot
in my left eye. I wonder if the poet who dressed as a cookie
is happy in his new marriage. I wonder if you can still get a bottle of Tab
anywhere, that awful soda my forever-dieting aunt used to drink,
with its pink logo, its *a* all swirls, looking like @.
                                        Yesterday,
when my husband was waiting at an intersection, he said, *Is anyone coming?* I
    looked from
the passenger seat and said confidently, *We can make it.*
Then we were almost run off the road. I said
I'm sorry I'm sorry through the exchange of honks and fists
and couldn't believe when my husband forgave me so quickly.

Not only that,
but I'm a bad proofreader, I thought to myself as I made a mental list
of ways that I felt inadequate. One friend also recently noted that maybe I
talk too much about myself, so I told her the Bette Midler joke,
Enough about me, what do you think of me? which doesn't *really*
bring me back to David Lehman and his poem, but does make me realize
how far away I strayed from my original point
which was that I thought his poem would be funny because of the title,
not the real title, but my mistaken one. I started to guess his poem
in my head: Pepsi is bubbly and brown while the Pope
is flat and white. Pepsi doesn't have a big white hat. The Pope
can't get rid of fender rust. Pepsi is all for premarital sex.
The Pope won't stain your teeth.
But "The Difference
Between Pepsi and Coke" is a tender poem about a father
whom the speaker reveres, and I wonder if David Lehman's own father
is alive or dead which is something I often do—wonder
how much is true—when I read a poem by someone I like
which I know is not the right way to read a poem even though
Molly Peacock said at her reading that she is the "I"
in all of hers and doesn't use the word "speaker" anymore.
Still,
I feel like a Peeping Tom, although this is really about what I can't see,
my blind spots, and how easy it is for me to doubt my decisions,
how I relate to the father in Lehman's poem who "won't admit his dread
of boredom" and panics and forgives. How easy it is to live for stretches at a time
in that skinny dark line, how easy it is to get so many things all wrong.

6

Lines

On our first date, instead of holding my hand, my future-husband looked
at my palm: *Here's your fame line   your heart line   the lucky M*
he said *you were in danger but you are coming out of it now.*
He said it like he meant it, the way the old women in the Philippines
had taught him. *Now make a fist   these two little lines under your pinky
these are the two kids you'll have.*
                                        My sister keeps waiting
for her third baby. She has three lines. Three kids, that's what the palm reader
at Rocky Point told her. *You'll get married next year
and you'll have three beautiful daughters.* My sister laughed and said
I'll get a second opinion because she was just a junior in high school
and sure she was going to college.
                                        On our first date my future-husband
    traced
the lines on my palm with his finger and I closed my hand around his
because it tickled. *If the pad near your thumb is fleshy,* he said,
it means you're very passionate. His own palms were chubby and pink,
his brown fingers tapered and elegant. He wore a silver and turquoise ring.
He said, *You'll get married only once*
                                        but later there'll be an affair.
Now that we're married, he can't find that wrinkle of infidelity.
Our palms change, he tells me, especially our right palms
that mutate through our behavior. He examines the bunch of tiny *x*s
that look like windshield frost, the wishbones, the spider webs,
the triangle dragon teeth.
                                        My sister will most likely have that third baby.
My husband sees those three lines though my sister groans,
Two are enough. Her oldest is already fourteen, and my sister
is finally able to start taking classes at the community college.
My husband says to make everyone feel better: *I was only kidding
I don't really know that much about predictions.*
                                        That night we all go
to Rocky Point which isn't as fun as it used to be, which is going bankrupt,
my sister says, like everything else in Rhode Island. The rollercoaster

is broken down, the cars off the tracks, lying on their sides
like cows. And hanging from the booths' roofs, giant Tweety Birds and Pink
    Panthers,
the cuddly neon elusive ones that hardly anyone ever wins.

The Little I Know about Eyes

That the image is reflected upside-down
before the brain switches it around
so we can see it. That if you cough too much
when you're little (let's say you have
asthma or bronchitis) your eye muscles
will feel the strain and one of your eyes
will become tired and you'll begin
to go cross-eyed (it happened to me)
but then if the doctor catches it in time
(like mine did) he'll put a patch
over the good eye to make the lazy one work
and even though you will still cough
this lazy eye will straighten itself out.
That we blink so fast so often
that we can't detect that blinking in others
with our own naked eyes that are also blinking.
That when I was little
kids teased the other kids who had to wear glasses
and called them four-eyes.
But that suddenly it became fashionable to wear glasses.
That people wearing glasses look smarter.
That contacts are very popular.
(My husband wears them.)
That you can be blind and still have
the most beautiful eyes.
That you shouldn't ever look
directly into the sun or at an eclipse.
That the disease commonly called "pink eye"
is technically conjunctivitis.
That a "red eye" flight will take you
from N.Y. to L.A. or vice versa overnight.
That when you close your eyes after staring
at an object you'll see its outline
in opposite colors.
That eyes produce eye snot

(what my aunt called it)
or sleepy seeds (what my mother-in-law
called it) especially when you have a cold.
That eyes get bloodshot when they don't rest enough.
That eyes are stolen out of some children
who live in El Salvador (I know this sounds
utterly impossible but it's true)
and sold for eye transplants in other countries.
That the children are kidnapped
like the British businessman was in New York—
he was kidnapped and drugged
and taken to some quack clinic
and then woke up the next day on a park bench in pain
because of the sloppy stitches.
That his kidneys had been stolen (this is all true—
I met a friend of this fellow at a party)
and organs are big sellers in certain parts of Asia
because it's against the law in certain countries
to donate your body to science.
That the eyes are taken from children
who will never see again.
That those children's eyelids will close
and fold into their eye sockets and they
will scare you for a minute when you look at them—
that is if they survive.
That I imagine most will die in the operation
because of the loss of blood and because
of the bad conditions under which it's performed.
That someone miles away
will pay good money for the eyes
of these children and use them as their own
(let's say the buyer has diabetes or glaucoma
or was born blind) and some of these eyes won't even take
because, after all, it's a difficult procedure
and there are no guarantees.
That someone you see on the street
may be looking at you with the eyes of a child
from El Salvador and not even know it.
That they may look away or squint to read small print.

That you may be farsighted or nearsighted or have astigmatism.
That it takes time for eyes to adjust
when you walk into a dark theater
and the movie's already started.
That you can't tell what you're buying anymore
just by looking at it with your eyes.

Happy Ending

I lost my virginity in a hotel
although on the police report I said it was stolen.
My virginity contained my only picture ID
and concert stubs that proved I'd seen Kiss and Queen.
I wanted it back. I wanted to slip my virginity
into my pocket where I'd last seen it,
the smooth red leather and jingling coin pouch,
the tight metal snap. I looked at each stranger
in the elevator—*Did you take it? Do you recognize me*
as the one you had for lunch? I sniffed the cubicle of air
for the scent of my sex on someone else. I sniffed
the lit buttons after each man had pushed one
hoping I'd left my smell on his hand. I finally went home
and wept, the blood on my panties three cherries
that won me nothing in the slot machine.
I watched a black and white TV, doodled on a hotel napkin
as my mother cried she didn't know me anymore.
I was grounded until the mail came several days later.
A kind stranger had sent me back my virginity
in a padded envelope so I could keep it
or lose it again, this time sober, with a boy my own age.
I checked the crotch of my panties I'd hidden under my bed.
The blood dots slid off like new pennies or cinnamon hearts,
then disappeared. My mother put down her iron and smiled,
braided my clean shiny hair as the whole world sang
a song about what a good girl I was.

Stranger

She looks so old now and gray as you tower over her
and remember, in certain clear flashes, she can't beat you anymore
which is kind of a ridiculous image—an elderly woman
whacking her grown married daughter, but then you think about
nursing homes and the abuse of the elderly—what it must be like
to bruise someone, on purpose, who was alive before the car was invented,
if it's the same rage that the mother you read about in the newspaper had
towards her crying baby when she picked him up and shook him
like he was a chicken in a clear plastic bag and she was trying to cover him
with all the spices that lay at the bottom, and she broke his neck, basically,
because he wasn't able to support his head yet, then she dropped him
back into the crib and ran for a long time, almost giddy with relief
and terror and guilt—what it must it be like to lift your hand to hurt someone
who is senile and babbling and spitting out the food you're trying to feed her.
Especially if you're the daughter and still hold this anger
tightly in your fist, like a sharp cloudy crystal, but now you're getting tender
because your hand hurts and you can only stay angry so long
because your mother's hair is now a gray tuft
and her eyes are so gluey and sweet and blank
she's not really even your mother anymore, but more like an old
boyfriend you think you see at the mall so you follow him
all the way to Coconut Records where he turns around
and almost steps on your foot—you're following him that close—
and he's scratching his head, wondering if he's missed the store
he wants to shop in, and when he spins around his face
is all wrong—it's not him, it's not him at all—and never
have you seen such a stranger as this man, as this aging woman before you
who laughs, then cries, then asks who you are, then calls you the wrong name
and you let her, so suddenly you're free from being her daughter
and you're in a place where there are no more bad parents, no ugly words,
just a big glowing rectangle and Muzak.

Grace

I stared at the floor, lifting up
the black tiles from the white. I could
do that, make flat surfaces
3-D by crossing my eyes. I could
spell anything, even words I didn't know
the definitions of—like "botulism"
and "claustrophobic" and "thyroid."
I'd close my eyes and letters would spill
like blocks and I'd get everything right
in the spelling bee. I'd know the exact
ages of people—41, 37, 56, 24—people
I'd never met, people who stopped by
Uncle Albert's big New Year's party
where I sat at the card table, beating
the old men at dominoes because I could see
how many dots were lying face down
so I always grabbed the ones I needed.
I understood foreign languages,
like French or Latin. I'd hear my Aunt Gigi
or the priest and I'd translate like
a pocket dictionary. I'd add up
three or four big numbers in a second
and a nearby adult was sure to kiss my forehead
or clap. I'd know the punch line
to jokes I was hearing the first time
and nothing much could scare me—
not the car that hit me when I was six,
my mother and her moods,
not the few things I couldn't predict.
I understood something bigger than the hums
that filled my ears like vacuums or
air-conditioners. I understood
if things got too bad I could die
if I had to, drink some bleach
when no one was watching.

I understood there were angels in my
thumb prints and sprites who lived
in my ear's hills who'd whisper
all the answers. I was full of confidence and will
as I plunged my hand into the cookie tin
filled with buttons and the first one
I grabbed was the same size
as the one that needed replacing.
I mean, that's just how I lived
until one New Year's I guessed
a 29-year-old-woman was fifty.
Her blue cat's-eye glasses threw me
and everyone laughed except the woman.
They laughed right over my begging
for a second chance. I fell
like a shooting star in slow motion,
one everyone gets to see and is
therefore unremarkable. The next week
I spelled dessert "desert" on a spelling bee.
Suddenly, ordinary.

How Much Is This Poem Going to Cost Me?

It's not something I like to burden my readers with as a rule,
the process of spending money for paper and paper clips, pens,
ink cartridges for the printer—never mind the computer itself
which is a whole other story.
                       My favorite uncle
was watching Phil Donahue—the topic was computers I guess—
and a journalist on the panel said, "No writer today
can live without one." My uncle called before the show was over
and offered to buy me my first computer. I dyed my hair red
for the first time, just days before he died. Some readers might think
that might be developed as a separate poem of its own, but since we're all
on tight budgets, I'll try to fit it in here:
                            How I called all night
and he wouldn't answer his phone. How my sister found him
early the next morning. The tension over his will.
How my mother picked me up at the train station for the funeral,
crying into my shoulder—her dead older brother
who brought her a hula skirt from the South Pacific after the war,
who gave her away at her wedding since their father
had already passed on—before she suddenly got a grip on herself and said:
"What the hell have you done to your hair?" My mother hates redheads
for some reason, always saying she would have drowned her kids
if any of them had been born strawberry blonde or auburn.
When I was little, my uncle used to live in the apartment downstairs.
That was before his wife died, very young,
so they never had a chance to have kids. He told me he felt helpless,
it was like watching a dying little bird...
                       I pay for this poem in many ways.
Right now, as I write this, I could be at a job earning money
or, at the very least, looking at the help-wanted ads. I could be writing
a screenplay, a novel that would maybe, just maybe, in the end pay for itself.
Sure "there are worse things I could do" as the slutty girl
sings in *Grease*, although it's not politically correct to call her that.
What do people say nowadays? Sexually daring?
I've always liked that character Rizzo—the way she finds out

she's not pregnant after all at the end of the movie,
calling her good news down to her friends
from the highest car on the Ferris wheel.
                                        I wish amusement parks
didn't have such high admission prices. And, of course, I still like to eat.
Why just this morning I had a big bowl of cereal. The box says
you can get sixteen servings, but my husband and I never get more than ten,
    which makes
each serving about forty cents, not including the milk
or the banana or the glass of juice. But without that fuel,
who says I could have written this same poem? It may have been shorter
and even sadder, because I would have had a hunger headache
and not given it my best.
                            Then there's rent. I can't write this poem outside
as there are no plugs for my computer, and certainly no
surge protectors. I need to be comfortable—a sweat shirt and sweat pants,
which used to be cheaper before everyone started getting into fitness.
I need my glasses more than ever as I get older.
Without insurance, I don't have to tell you how expensive they are.
I need a pair of warm socks and a place to sleep.
Dreams are very important to poets. I need recreation, escape, Hollywood
    movies.
You may remember I made reference to one earlier called *Grease,*
lines 32–38 of this very poem.
                                It's not easy,
now that movies in New York are eight seventy-five.
You get in the theater and smell the buttered popcorn,
though everyone knows it's not really butter they use.
It's more like yellow-colored lard. Any poet with heart trouble
best skip it. But my husband and I smell it
and out come our wallets. The concession stand uses so much salt
every movie goer also needs a drink, and everyone knows
what those prices are like. We say goodbye to another twenty bucks,
but that's just the beginning—
there are envelopes, bottles of Bic Wite-Out, stamps, and disks.

Bangungot

Ever since my husband told me about *bangungot*
and taught me how to say it—
three short nasally syllables, a cross between
banana and coconut—I've been worried
he's going to get it, that he'll die in his sleep.
Some Filipinos believe a demon sits on a man's chest
or violent nightmares are the real killers.
My husband thinks it's too much
fish sauce or shrimp paste late at night,
that third helping of rice. *Bangungot*
strikes men 25–40, men who like to eat
then snooze. I try not to let my husband do this
and suggest, instead of television, a walk after dinner,
a game of cards. But sometimes I have places to go.
Sometimes I fall asleep before he does.
It's then I dream of my husband's stomach—
a pot of rice boiling over, a banana so ripe
its own skin cracks. Or I fly, just from the waist up,
a *manananggal,* a vampire that can only be killed
with salt, a vampire who kills men in their sleep.
The top of my body leans into my husband's chest
and I demand he teach me to pronounce the word
that doesn't look like it's spelled. He is confused,
asks me *Where are your legs?*
By the time I get them back,
I'm a widow in black ballerina flats.

Insomnio

I wonder how I ended up here in Mojácar, Spain, how I swam in the
Mediterranean on my birthday. How I became so lucky and blessed—and
terrified so I can't sleep. How I came to a place known as "the city of witches,"
where there might be in this quiet dead of night a witch-ceremony somewhere
that I am not invited to, since I am just a tourist. The guidebook says there
still are such gatherings on sheltered corners of mountainsides. I've heard Tia
Cachocha can still cure lovesickness with her powders called *pichirichis*. Tia
Carrica is best at spells and knows how to cure the evil eye, which you know
you have when your favorite foods start tasting bad and you're consumed with
a melancholy brought on by nothing you can name. Carrica's remedy is the
leaves of nine poisonous plants and special prayers. St. Teresa takes the sickness
out of your mind. St. Clement works on headaches. The Virgin Mary works
miracles for your stomach. I wonder if the spells work and why. I wonder if
the folds of my brain look like the folds of my bowels, that same slippery gray.

I was so angry when Henry said *Wow, you're really smart, I'm surprised* after
he read my essay. I said *You thought I was an idiot?* and he said *Well, you say
"like" a lot. You're kind of silly.* And I remember thinking *What can I do to make
myself more serious in appearance?* But I never did anything. I had so many
plans in my life that I never followed through on. It's weird. I think I'm the
opposite of Henry's perception. I think I'm even stupider than what I convey.
My musings about death might be clever if coming from a teenager, but from
me, they seem rather obvious. I read books, even philosophy, and when I'm
in the grips of an idea, when I understand it in my gut, I feel transported,
transformed, a stringent intelligence, like ammonia washing out my cerebral
cortex. But then I close the book and watch TV or start cooking dinner or
answer the phone and everything is lost—I can't remember a thing, and in a
year or two, I'm just any old schmuck who says: *Yeah, I read that book. But I
can't remember how it ends.*

If I could only capture the moment I fall asleep, then I wouldn't be so afraid
of death. That slick lizard that's under a rock before you know it, that screen-
blip, that lip that's warm, then cold, then gone.

Sometimes I think *I'm here* and am amazed at my own breathy sounds and hard teeth.

Sometimes I write terrible fortunes for imaginary cookies: *Someone at this table knows your secret.* I write them on tiny pieces of paper that I imagine would fit in the innards of the cookie's crescent: *The affair you are contemplating will ruin your life.* Or something like: *Your happiest days happened a long time ago.* Then I think of the fortune teller in Milton, PA, in jail for fraud. She conned someone out of forty-thousand dollars and none of her predictions even came true. Her customer must have been embarrassed to take her to court, to admit to the judge that she believed in lighting candles and using love potions to try to keep her husband home. And the judge, what did he think? Did he make snide remarks to the woman who lost the money? Those kind of cruel innuendoes smart people are so good at they can't stop themselves, even when they know they are acting wrongly, obnoxiously superior. I wonder if I've seen either woman, the fortune teller or her customer, at Weis Market or Roy's Bakery. I wonder what they look like.

My mother pulled my thumb out of my mouth and said *Smell this.* She held my wet thumb to my nose and I said *Smells like Fish & Chips* which it did. She wanted to shame me into straight teeth, and sleep that's independent of sucking, but I put my thumb in my mouth whenever she was out of view, when I was in front of the TV, when I was sitting on the toilet. I peeled the skin off of my lips in tiny pink flakes. I like to see kids sucking their thumbs now in strollers, the faraway look they have in their eyes if their eyes are open, and I wonder if I'll hear a sucking noise when I die, if it will be totally dark except for those tongue/saliva/swallowing sounds, if I'll know enough to follow them, if I'll suck with my soul-lips towards heaven.

My husband's skin is warm, like milk heated just right in a bottle. In minutes, he can heat the whole bed, better than an electric blanket. I wonder if it's something spiritual, this warmth in his hands that knead my back when it's sore and seem to heal it, or if it's high blood pressure or something dangerous. My husband doesn't know his medical history since he was adopted, doesn't know the time he was born, so he can't have his exact astrology chart done, not that he wanted one, but I thought it would be helpful, an instruction manual for me to better understand him. I couldn't believe when I heard there was a newly-discovered thirteenth house, but it makes sense, when you think of it—

how astrology is almost right, but usually off in some fundamental way. Soon all these astrology books will be obsolete.

When husbands and wives who are Mormon die, they have secret passwords to say to each other so that they'll be able to seek each other out, since they won't have their earthly bodies to recognize each other with. Or maybe that is just a very secular translation of a more sacred truth. But it's interesting to think about, how we'll recognize each other later, if there is a whole new language to learn after death, if we'll start over again with big note books and strict grammar school teachers, how we'll hear without ears. In Mojácar, shepherds know the exact place to stand, when the air currents are best so they can shout to their friends all the way on the next mountain. Sometimes, by mistake, conversations get carried to the wrong place, so southern Spain has a lot of good gossip. Sneezes have been known to ricochet off four or five buildings and startle the goats who run into an olive grove.

Sometimes my body feels tiny and I imagine its insignificance, for instance, when I think of what kind of telescope someone in outer space would need to find my house and then focus into the right window and see me among all my things, like the bureaus and paintings. Sometimes my body feels huge, like it is too big for the bed and the rest of the world is small and faraway in perspective. Sometimes I like to get up in the middle of the night and try on a dress that I haven't worn in a long time, just to see if it fits, to see if it looks different now that my hair has grown longer. Sometimes my fall back to sleep is sudden.

Sometimes I am the paramecium shapes I see when I close my eyes, the pale blue lightning, the orange squiggles.

The Therapist's Funeral

for Rodney Godden

One definition of jet lag is the process of a soul
trying to catch up with a body—which makes sense
for the living whose souls probably haven't evolved to flying
as fast as the jets that carry them, so they fall behind
swirling first with clouds, then rain
that mingles with exhaust from another plane.
For all we know, a similar process happens when you die,

except there's no body you're trying to catch up with
and maybe you're glad. You're heaven-bound
and is that up or down or into a flower's core?
I hope your soul is on time, wherever it is,
getting where it's supposed to. I hope it isn't
an *alma en pena,* what the Mexicans call a lost soul,
drifting among heaven's custom inspectors,

fumbling, with none of the right papers. Even if you
lost faith just before you died—which can happen,
even to saints and folks like Jesus—I hope
you're finding it again, getting used to the time change,
the weather not really weather at all. The ticking accents
and strange currency. All those dead relatives crowding in
for photos, some of whom your soul barely even remembers.

Be gentle with yourself, maybe heaven's therapists say,
just like the therapists on earth. *This is a time of transition.* Your
soul might not be able to read the road signs at first
or get comfy in that strange soft bed. The new food
not what your soul is used to. No phone, no postcards, no stamps, just
a small boat—your neck, shoulders, spine dissolving. You knew more
about me than anyone, but you're quickly forgetting.

White Virgin

a statue of Mary in Toledo, Spain

She's the only smiling Virgin known to the world.

Jesus has His Mother's hair and a little wise smirk
as He cups Mary's chin in His palm.
It's a private moment, telepathic and almost Oedipal,
if it weren't for the fact that God was already out
of the picture, an absentee Father. And Joseph
could barely count, always away under contract
for this or that Bethlehem housing project.
Mary's lost all the weight from her pregnancy,
gotten herself back into shape. Jesus enjoys
the way the skin on her face
feels like the most expensive of fabrics.

We can't let them know we like to have fun,
Jesus gurgles. Mary hears His words
even though her Son is too young to speak.
She doesn't call the aunts or her friends to brag
about Jesus's first words because she's used to
strange occurrences. Every once in a while
she even hears what the animals say.
She's seen an angel. She's had a kid without doing it.
She will take instructions from anyone
she trusts, even a talking infant.

From now on Mary closes the windows
whenever she has the urge to tickle, or blow
on Jesus's sweet naked belly.
From now on the Saviour and His Mom
keep their giddy goo-gah playing times to themselves.
They have quite a few years to go before things get rough.
When they pose for the rest of the artists,
they bite the insides of their cheeks

or think of the saddest of things,
like wars and injustices and heathens.
Because they share so many private jokes,
they have to be careful not to burst out laughing.

Art

Because I was brought up in a working class family
I used to resent poems with references to supposedly famous paintings
which I'd never heard of or seen. Not that working class people
are excluded from looking at paintings, it's just that my family never went
to a museum except for the Museum of Science after our jaunt
to the Boston Aquarium. Then one day after I'd been to college
and read a lot of books and went to the Southwest,
I wrote a poem about Georgia O'Keeffe
and I thought, well, that's not too bad, since you can buy O'Keeffe
calendars and postcards in Job Lot, a discount store
in the town I grew up in. I justified my poem since
Georgia was pretty famous by now. And Renoir was OK,
since everyone had heard of him even if they hadn't seen his work,
or Keith Haring since his paintings wound up on buttons and tee shirts
and advertisements for vodka. Or Andy Warhol
since there was a book about him in the window displays of mall bookstores
and, after he died, gossip on TV about the fights over his estate.
But I didn't think it was OK to write about El Greco or Velazquez or Goya
since you had to go to Madrid or Barcelona to see most of their paintings
and most poets write about their experience of seeing the real thing
as opposed to seeing reproductions in a book. But then I met my husband
who loved art and could name periods and influences and who studied under
    whom.
His life had been a fairy tale and he took me in without condition
like all Princes who marry Cinderellas do. He told me his story,
how he was dropped from his furry nest
near a rice plantation into the crib of a mansion
where his new parents were so happy to see him
they bought him a sombrero and a mini-guitar
and the maids fought over who would be the lucky one able to change his diaper
and powder his sweet rump. He took me to Spain and showed me
what his father had shown him on all his childhood trips
from the Philippines to Europe. All the men
in El Greco's paintings had small heads and long dark bodies,
his trademark the hands with middle fingers stuck together. And I knew

28

I could write a poem about "Las Meninas" because Velazquez
had ambivalence about the rich like I did and tried to show them
in a rather unflattering light. But who in my family would know "Las Meninas,"
the self-portrait with the trick of the mirror and innovations
in perspective? Who in my town had been to the Prado?
Who wanted to go even if they could? I stood near Goya's nightmares
and shadows, the tour guide speaking first in Spanish, then in English.
My husband had started out poorer than I had, before he was adopted,
but now he was confident, looking at the small details
of a witch's bloody teeth, contemplating each brush stroke and meaning.
Oh Velazquez, I want to go back to your work in the other wing,
the portraits of midgets and jesters painted with the same dignity as royalty.
You knew how so much about luck and money
are accidents of birth, how magical and unfair it all is.
I crumpled my admissions ticket then smoothed it out,
my ticket I'd press behind the plastic flap in my scrap book
not to show anyone in my family back home
but just for me, to remind myself that I was both, still
and no longer, who I once was.

Nick at Nite

When growing up, Nick never saw *The Brady Bunch*.
He watched *Eat Bulaga* with Tito, Vic, and Joey,
which he likens to a Filipino version of *The Three Stooges*.
He ate Sky Flakes crackers instead of Ritz
and drank Royal True Orange with pulp bits instead of Sunkist.
He remembers the bells signalling the after-dinner arrival
of Magnolia ice cream—vendors pushing silver coolers,
not driving trucks. I tell him about Apple Jacks,
the cereal that turned a kid's milk pink
and the phenomenon of Banana Quik.
I try to explain Madge, the brassy beautician who dipped
her clients' hands in Palmolive Dishwashing Liquid
between manicures. My husband endures
the moving scrapbook of my childhood
as we watch another round of Nick at Nite.
I teach him all the words to the *Patty Duke Show* theme song
during a break from their sponsors Head & Shoulders.
In the Philippines, dandruff was also an embarrassment.
Nick tells me of a shampoo commercial in English and Tagalog:
A girl loses interest in her dancing partner
when she notices the white patches on his collar
and huffs away as only the truly insulted can.
The famous slogan: "Charlie Balakubak, excuse me!"
My husband and I laugh. We are "East Meets West"
like LaChoy, makers of "Oriental recipes to serve at home."
I sing him "*Aye, yie, yie-yie* . . . I am the Frito Bandito."
Nick, who only started speaking English at six,
translates the original Spanish lyrics. The song, he says,
is really about singing without tears, not the virtues of corn chips.

Where to Find Feminine Protection While Traveling in a Foreign Country

Your tampons won't be near the diapers in Madrid's famous El Corte Inglés.
Or near the deodorants or near the shampoos. You'll search the back walls
of the store because you're used to such items out of view in the States
and because you're too embarrassed to ask—besides, how do you say
sanitary napkin in Spanish? In Turre, in the South, the women believe
in always wearing pants when they're having their periods. Lizards
have been known to sniff them out and scurry up and underneath skirts
because they love the warm blood that's thicker and browner
than anything succulent in the desert. Women must be careful
when they turn over the rocks in their gardens,
when they stretch to pinch the figs in their orchards. A lizard
wants to suck a woman dry until its sucking causes such pain
that the woman must soak a slice of bread in hot water
and put it on her stomach. Hopefully the lizard will mistake
the bread on her belly for a rock that's been in the sun
and crawl out of her vagina and lounge there.
I still have a few days left to find pads, according to my calendar,
but I've started to feel that swell in my breasts that makes my bra
too tight a few days at the end of every month, that swell my sister says
is even more pronounced when your period never comes
because you're pregnant. I've always been afraid of such a severe change
in the body and the women in Turre agree, explaining they're most vulnerable
after the baby comes. Snakes love the taste of human breast milk
and men have been known to guard the front doors of their houses
while mothers are feeding their babies. Snakes are the only ones
in Turre who don't sleep through siesta so new mothers should nap
on their stomachs, cupping the sides of their breasts with their hands
so the snakes will not be able to slip under them. Even when her baby's lips
are surrounding her nipple, a woman in Turre pays close attention.
She doesn't watch a talk show or chat with her friend on the phone—
snakes are quiet and fast. Some have been known to coil
their bodies around feeding babies and gag infant mouths
with their serpent tails. Snakes have their sucking perfected

so their mouths can imitate the power and rhythms
of the smallest of children. And as much as she might want to cry,
all the baby can do is rub her gums against the cool snake skin filling her mouth.
You'll never believe where they keep the tampons in El Corte Inglés in Madrid.
Just as I'd given up and was about to leave, I saw them in a row under the
     front counter
where the gum and mints would be in an American pharmacy. I chose an exotic
French brand, *Ausonia Seda,* scented, with wings. The feminine protection
was opposite the pastry counter displaying cream puffs and fruit tarts, right
     across
from the Godiva chocolates, their gold foil boxes secured with gold foil string.

Cockroaches

That's what my father-in-law calls the American kids
who scamper through Europe each summer
with their backpacks and Eurail passes, some of them
even honeymooning, he says, disgusted. Such a small wardrobe,
such unattractive luggage. I don't tell him that I was a cockroach
fifteen Junes ago, making 300 American dollars last a whole month,
eating *arroz con pollo* four nights in a row in the cheapest restaurant
in Barcelona, that I washed my underwear in *pension* sinks.
I can't tell him these things because he is old
and elegant, embarrasses easily, knows about tax

shelters and Deutsche marks and yen. Besides, he shares
what he has with me. O.K. It's true—technically
cockroaches are most active in summer months, but some believe
they can also cure skin ulcers when ground and mixed with sugar.
Scientists have just invented tiny video cameras
they can strap onto roaches who crawl through earthquake debris
and enemy hotel rooms, unnoticed, the perfect rescue workers and spies.
They were here on earth before we were, they'll likely
survive a nuclear attack. Most often cockroaches die on their backs.
I know this from the ones I lived with in New York City tenements.

You can kill roaches with mashed potatoes laced with arsenic,
or with black plastic discs full of poison. I hated them even before
I saw my first one. Roaches—that's what we called the boys next door
whose last name was Rochelle, whose father was a circus clown
with a bad temper when his make-up was off, whose above-the-ground
pool perched in their driveway—the dirty water, pea soup
thickened with a ham hock. *"La cucaracha, la cucaracha,"*
my sister and I sang as the younger brother peed
into their cat's litter box. Then he'd chase after us, trying
to pee on our new red Keds. My mother said,

"Keep away from those kids. They're full of lice
and trashy ideas." So how I saw the Rochelles was how

my husband's father would have seen me then: poking my tongue
through my missing front tooth, wearing a hand-me-down tee shirt
from my cousin that read "Sock it to me, baby,"
a phrase that had peaked in popularity a few years before.
My father and mother passing each other every day at three,
one working first, the other second shift. Hamburger Helper
and Coolwhip. We were cockroaches, happy as all the rest,
scurrying fast across the dirty tub we knew as America.

Fairy Tale

One morning a kindly working class woman
found a tree in her backyard that grew real money. She pinched
twenty dollar bills from a couple of stems
before she finished hanging out her wash and heading to work.
She woke up her lazy unemployed husband to show him—
big mistake. He tried to get his wife to call her boss and quit.
But how could she plant all her hopes on a grow-rich-scheme?
The couple had a quick argument about whether to contact
the local TV station or the government, then decided
to tell no one until she came home at six. She didn't know
her husband would pluck off all the money while she was at the factory
and the tree would slump over and die. He made $2,000 altogether,
which would have been more if he'd waited for all the money to ripen.
No store would take the small bitter bills he'd picked too soon.
He left them in the fruit basket by the yellowing bananas,
but the tiny money was the dark green of thwarted cherries.
Instead of buying his wife a present, the husband treated his pals
to lunch at the local diner, then gave the rest of his money
to his cousin who was always in debt—
"like us" the wife reminded him, but her husband was already asleep
on the couch, his belly full of the daily special, corned beef hash.
Crying, the wife searched their back yard for seeds,
but the big rich birds had somehow found out about the tree.
Dollars in their beaks, they flew away. They'd eaten absolutely everything.

Surgery

I sleep for so many days like a princess who's eaten poison
except my waking is slow and kissless and the woman with four arms
keeps visiting my dreams, swirling scarves around my middle,
and the woman with four legs hides her secret, two small feet dangling
from the short snake legs under her skirt. The Penguin Girl
and Dog-Faced Boy point to my scar and say *what's so bad about that—*
a mosquito bite scratch, a paper cut. The smallest woman in the world
sits in my hand wearing her nineteenth century dress. My pillows
become the fat lady's breasts and I am Alice, first big and then small.

The doctor comes and I won't look as he changes the gauze
and says *the swelling's going down* and *it looks good.* It's not really true
that the Elephant Man's mother was knocked down by elephants
just before he was born. I wonder why no one marveled at his perfectly shaped
penis, his pure desire, no woman to love him. I wonder if we are all
really animals, our shock of pubic hair more like fur than anything else,
that dark patch hailing back to a time before speech. Nothing comes out
when I scream right after the operation and for a moment I have no language.
Though I want to say *help me,,* I can only think in visuals, raw and red.

The nurse comes by and says *I know it hurts honey* and suddenly
the rows of stretchers begin to moan in the thin cloudy light of the recovery room
and the dolphin arches over me—she's beautiful, gray metal and clear liquid
like IV fluid—and Koko the gorilla remembers her parents
being captured and she tells the humans in sign language and begins to cry.
The nurse says the operation's worked—*you're going to have a baby, the first*
baby to be part human, part ape. I'm so happy I begin to laugh,
which triggers a ball of brown fur and blood to spill, easy as urine,
as the doctor shakes his sad head. When I wake again

to the TV hum, a gorilla is saving a child who's fallen
into a zoo exhibit. I stare at the limp boy and stick my hand into the bowl
of melted ice on my tray. I find a small cold sliver and rub it
to my chapped lips. If I could reach the TV knobs, I'd turn up the volume.

If I could reach the phone, I'd call my mother. I can't walk so the electronic cuffs
massage my calves and the massage feels good — up and down, one leg at a time.
The fish between my legs swims in a squiggle and I push the button
for another squirt of morphine — my incision begins to chatter,
then floats through the gauze, above the sheets, a full set of the tiniest possible
     teeth.

Scared about What Was There

I started my period the day before seventh grade, which in most American towns is the first grade in junior high. Woonsocket's junior high was so bad it was called The Zoo. I tried to wear the right thing, which I thought was a red mini-skirt with a red blazer. But since my mother sewed most of our clothes and she'd run out of material, this blazer had short puffy sleeves. I wore saddle shoes, except it was the seventies so these particular ones had platform soles made of red sponge. My pantyhose were a dark shade because I thought this way my legs would look tanned—they were a shiny brand on the advice of my best friend who said such a style made our legs look thinner. Sanitary pads then were held up by belts and Modess had tabs of gauze in the front and back that had to be worked elaborately into the metal belt hooks, not unlike tightening the straps on your back pack or those that lead to the bib of your overalls.

I was kind of a skinny thirteen-year-old since I ate only half of everything on my plate ever since I started getting breasts, so those Modess pads seemed huge under my skirt, and I was sure everyone knew I was menstruating. I went to the bathroom between every class, and I was careful not to squirm in my seat because who knew which way that sanitary napkin could slide, riding up my back or up towards my belly. I don't remember if I had pubic hair yet, or how much. I never saw any of it grow in—I didn't look down until I was sixteen and even then I was surprised and a little scared about what was there.

My sister didn't know about periods since she was a year younger, and I was amazed that we would go into public toilets at the movies or in restaurants and she would walk right by that white metal machine with the rusted corners that was stuck to the wall like a medicine cabinet, that she wouldn't notice the ad with that woman with the blond swept-up hair smelling daisies, who was serenely menstruating, taking the week off to spend in a field.

My mother complained that I went through too many pads, that I should wait a few hours before changing them. She held up the baby blue box and said *I can't afford to have you go through one of these a day.* I didn't like the squish between my legs and feared gushes like urine when I least expected them. It took me a long time to trust my mother who promised that wouldn't happen, to find my rhythm: the first two days heavy, the third day the cramps, the fourth day nearly gone, the blood coming back one more day on the fifth. My grandmother had to use strips of cotton cloth then wash them in cold water, chapping her hands, her mother dying before her period came so that when she had her first she ran into the barn screaming, sure she was dying too and refused to tell her father what was wrong. She said she sat there with the animals, a horse she usually took care of licking her cheeks. She held onto a lamb, she petted the sheep until her father figured out what was happening, but had no idea what to say. He called upon an aunt, who snipped the corners of an old bed sheet then tore it into squares my grandmother could fold and pin into the crotch of her bloomers. *You girls have it so lucky these days,* she told me, rather shyly, just before she died, just before the first tampon TV commercials, just before the lucky pairing of sanitary napkins and adhesive.

I'm Dealing with My Pain

He's about 300 pounds and knows martial arts, boxing, and wrestling—both the real and the fake kind. So I never know when I'm thrown to the ground or hurled against the ropes of a boxing ring fence (who can guess when he'll surprise me with a punch next?) if the ache in my back is real or cartoon, if my bruises will stay or wash off like kiddie tattoos.

Pain is a sneak and a cheat. He loves to eat unhealthy foods (scrapple, greasy gravy, Little Debbie Snacks). Not only that—I think he smokes. I can smell it on his breath, all fire and ash, when he pins me to my bed without asking. He's hefty and invisible and likes to strike in the dark so that even my magnifying glass and double locks are useless. Sometimes I call him Sumo, the Devil, or any member of my family. He's a changeling and a scam. His footprints are the ones that make cracks in the sidewalk.

Pain first introduced himself as a sadist. I was confused at the time. He said he was seduced by the blue of my wrists, the soft hollow at the center of my throat. He squeezed my heart like a Nerf ball until it was all lumps and fingernail marks. I nursed Pain like a mother. I tried to cheer him up like a sister, but everyone knows how that story goes.

Pain and I did have a few good times, if you can call them that. Eating ice cream under the covers, our tears drying on our cheeks so they chapped. We liked to go to movies alone. Pain, being invisible, snuck in without paying, then he'd leave the seat next to mine and feel up another girl in the theater. I could always tell which one. I'd hear her crying the way I did or crunching her popcorn as though each kernel was a small bone in Pain's neck or foot. He still comes around, though I tell him it's over, though I spit into his round hairy face.

He just laughs that sexy laugh. You know, the kind that gets in your head and you can't tell if it's making you nauseous or turning you on. There's no restraining order that works on Pain, the outlaw who loves to chase and embrace us, the outlaw we sometimes love to chase and embrace.

Tulip

This is what the fashion magazine said:
if you must eat pasta, you should never eat more
than a tulip-sized amount, your meat never bigger
than a deck of cards. I was ashamed of my past—
my big bowl of noodles with butter melted on top,
two dozen tulips at least, enough pasta for a month
if I were a *Cosmo* girl, if I could wear dresses
as small as nickels, if my feet were peas.
I never told my husband that I ate the last slice
of our two-year-old wedding cake after a fight
and it's amazing: you don't die, even if the cake is icy
and the frozen frosting flakes away like dry skin
and you're eating really old flour and eggs
when you think about it, but I didn't think about it
or wait for the cake to defrost. I did tell a few people
about the lawn chair I threw at him later
and another friend said, "That's not so bad.
I threw a jar of jam at my boyfriend."
My husband never asked about the missing cake
that lived in foil, behind the ice cubes, for so long.

House-Sitting

She lies on her girlfriend's bed looking at the pictures in her girlfriend's husband's *Playboy*. The big artificial breasts like glazed holiday breads on the cover of *Family Circle*. It's all the same: the body varnish that glistens women and turkeys, that sells them. This is how she feels about it politically anyway—angry, threatened, misrepresented. But her clit begins rising against her will, like a new tooth through resistant gum and she hates her body for being aroused, her own skin soft and spread, a dull white finish, poultry before it's cooked, something no one would want to buy or eat.

She looks at these airbrushed computerized pin-ups, fleshy robots, pouting like she never sees anyone pout on the street. Even though they are all the same, she likes some of them more than others, their ass cheeks smooth as marbles, forgiving her for her own, lumpy as golf balls. She tries to imagine their personalities, maybe some are smart or funny or clumsy.

She cannot quite dream she is one of them as she lies on those thick quilts, with her girlfriend's red high heels and her girlfriend's husband's denim work shirt. She cannot quite dream that she's lying above a caption for phone sex: *I'm wet, I'm horny, give me a call.* And she knows she couldn't enjoy touching such rubbery slick skin which looks as though it would be cold and indifferent, like the pages of the magazine itself. What is the proper response of a woman looking at *Playboy*? Why did she bring it with her to lie on the bed? Is her friend upset with her husband when he does? Why does her whole body blush, her stomach warm—one mouth a little wet, the other a little dry.

She hadn't looked at a magazine like this since sixth grade, for which anyone would have forgiven her. But now, as a grown woman, why does she touch one of her own breasts, losing, for just a second, her disappointment in its lack of firmness, still looking at the Bunnies—all cupcakes and maraschino cherries—stomachs as flat as Pop Tarts, their fingernails, little pink wings. She parts the hair that tangles over her vulva. Her orgasm is quick and salty, forgettable as fast food. What she does with the magazine is what she guesses any man does—put it back exactly where it was hidden, then sleep away the guilt, the shame.

Sex with a Famous Poet

I had sex with a famous poet last night
and when I rolled over and found myself beside him I shuddered
because I was married to someone else,
because I wasn't supposed to have been drinking,
because I was in a fancy hotel room
I didn't recognize. I would have told you
right off this was a dream, but recently
a friend told me, *write about a dream,*
lose a reader and I didn't want to lose you
right away. I wanted you to hear
that I didn't even like the poet in the dream, that he has
four kids, the youngest one my age, and I find him
rather unattractive, that I only met him once,
that is, in real life, and that was in a large group
in which I barely spoke up. He disgusted me
with his disparaging remarks about women.
He even used the word "Jap"
which I took as a direct insult to my husband who's Asian.
When we were first dating, I told him
"You were talking in your sleep last night
and I listened, just to make sure you didn't
call out anyone else's name." My future-husband said
that he couldn't be held responsible for his subconscious,
which worried me, which made me think his dreams
were full of blond vixens in rabbit-fur bikinis,
but he said no, he dreamt mostly about boulders
and the ocean and volcanoes, dangerous weather
he witnessed but could do nothing to stop.
And I said, "I dream only of you,"
which was romantic and silly and untrue.
But I never thought I'd dream of another man—
my husband and I hadn't even had a fight,
my head tucked sweetly in his armpit, my arm
around his belly, which lifted up and down

all night, gently like water in a lake.
If I passed that famous poet on the street,
he would walk by, famous in his sunglasses
and blazer with the suede patches at the elbows,
without so much as a glance in my direction.
I know you're probably curious about who the poet is,
so I should tell you the clues I've left aren't
accurate, that I've disguised his identity,
that you shouldn't guess *I bet it's him* . . .
because you'll never guess correctly
and even if you do, I won't tell you that you have.
I wouldn't want to embarrass a stranger
who is, after all, probably a nice person,
who was probably just having a bad day when I met him,
who is probably growing a little tired of his fame—
which my husband and I perceive as enormous,
but how much fame can an American poet
really have, let's say, compared to a rock star
or film director of equal talent? Not that much,
and the famous poet knows it, knows that he's not
truly given his due. Knows that many
of these young poets tugging on his sleeve
are only pretending to have read all his books.
But he smiles anyway, tries to be helpful.
I mean, this poet has to have some redeeming qualities, right?
For instance, he writes a mean iambic.
Otherwise, what was I doing in his arms.

Skipping Breakfast

I've turned into my Grammy, someone who glorifies the Depression, except I glorify my one tangy year of unemployment, that one bright flash of staying in my pajamas every day until four. Reading and writing all morning and afternoon. I've heard people say there's such a thing as a writing disease, that if certain people don't get their ideas down they'll go crazy, like the woman in *The Yellow Wallpaper*. I can relate except I'm so busy with my new teaching job that I'm not even sure if there's wallpaper in my new apartment. I come home, slump on the couch, try to read something I want to read, then fall asleep.

When I was unemployed I watched *Oprah* every day at four. Now I don't know what's going on in the world, yesterday's newspaper still fat and crisp on my desk. I heard about that circus elephant who'd had enough and trampled his owner and some kids in the crowd only about a week after it happened. I will soon be that elephant if I don't get any time off. But it's hard to say that to the boss when all he'd have to do is place one little ad and hundreds of applicants would be waiting in line for my position. It's like being jealous and protective of a husband you don't even love, this feeling of clinging I have to my job.

I know what you're thinking (especially if you're my mother): *What a brat, everyone has to work. You think I like my job? You think I wouldn't rather be home watching my soaps?* Perhaps I shouldn't have told you about *Oprah*—I swear she was all I watched with any regularity, *Oprah* and *Roseanne*. I'd go back and revise that other line if I had time, if this were the old days and I was just writing about what I thought it would feel like to have a hectic job. Then, I would have worked on this poem at my leisure. Reread it hundreds of times, tinkering until I had all the right nuances. Now I barely have twenty more minutes before I have to start getting ready for work, and that's if I compromise and go with wet hair.

This poem means I'm skipping breakfast, that I set my alarm an hour early. The other thing I hate, more than the teaching, more than the meetings, more than the politics which are as complicated as Bosnia, are the shoes. My sweet year of unemployment, I had soft feet, nestled in warm socks all day. My toes went braless and never once did my breasts know the snug laces of winter boots. Now I'm confined for all those hours at the chalkboard, at the desk.

The one time I took my blazer and headband off, the dean knocked on my office door to see how I was getting along. I answered as though he'd woken me out of bed, my hair all wild static, my silk shirt sliding out of my pants' waist. How can I write my poems wearing watches and belts? How can I even grade papers that way?

I think the anxiety I feel about my job may also be complicated by "time disease." I read about it in a book on quantum physics. Well, it was actually more like a self-help/quantum physics book. OK, it wasn't even mine, it belonged to my best friend, and I only read that one "time" chapter. See, I'm a fraud, and that's how I feel when I'm teaching.

Someone might argue that this isn't even a poem and label it an essay which I would have to defend by saying something as flimsy as "Only in poems may toes wear brassieres." But what do I really know about distinguishing between genres? Prosepoems are the look-alike cousins of the shortest short stories. What do I really know about Keats except that he used, with great success, the occasional terminal trochee. Except that he didn't live very long. He could have also had this time disease, in addition to TB, which manifests itself when a person thinks they only have a certain amount of time to live, so they die exactly right after what the doctor tells them they're allotted. For example, if I tell myself I'll never finish this poem in my remaining ten minutes, I won't. Not even a rough draft.

But it's even more complicated than that. The book says people who fear they don't have time to finish specific tasks, bring on all that stress with them, stress that eventually kills them. Their heart rate is irregular, their colon sluggish, as it rebels against the hyperactivity of all other organs. So, I don't know, perhaps you are reading this very fast because you have an appointment and you don't want to be late. That self-help chapter would tell you slow down, breathe, all spondee, and short lines, and excess punctuation. But I'm telling you I understand. I'm telling you we'd both better run.

Another Poem Called "Sphincter"

A minister writes a letter to the dean
asking that I be fired for teaching pornography
to his daughter who is a junior in college.
The pornography in question is Allen Ginsberg's
poem "Sphincter" from the anthology
Poets for Life. I'm so upset I can't sleep.
My husband cradles me like I'm pudding
and he's the dish. His cock
is close to the puckered bottle-cap rim of my anus
that leads to a place as dark as root beer.
Until now I've never referred to my husband's penis
as a cock or written so blatantly about my own anus
in a poem. It's probably because I'm rebelling
and trying to shock that minister
who helps put up billboards of cartoon fetuses
that say "Stop Abortion Now!" My friend's daughter
needs one this weekend and she will have to
cower through the protesters, keeping the collar
of her jacket up and over her face. It was a hard
decision. She went back and forth, whether
she should have a baby or finish school. I've never
had an abortion, still, I like the idea that I could
if I needed to. I like Allen Ginsberg's poem
even though I've never liked the idea of anal sex.
I think for me, and maybe the minister,
it's because when you think of anal sex
you have to think of shit which makes me,
and maybe the minister, self-conscious
and uncomfortable because we live in a society
with air fresheners and flushing toilets.
We're not like those pre-industrial kings
who defecated with pride in the most ornate
porcelain bowls. What an honor it was
for the most beloved servant to carry the waste away.

We're not even how we were as babies
when we thought the soft shapes in our diapers
were beautiful sculptures. Maybe it is rather taboo
to talk about sphincters in a college classroom.
Maybe it is even a sin—cocks, like missionaries,
going into places where they don't belong. I can't believe
I have to work tomorrow and face that student
who wears a sweatshirt which reads *I'm single* on the front—
but never alone. Christ is always with me!
on the back. My husband says,
"Let it go, you've got to get some sleep."
His cock is as hard as a block of cheddar cheese.
It rests against the left cheek of my ass.
I hope that doesn't offend you, dear reader,
unless you are the minister who wrote the letter
to the dean. I like imagining that minister
has a secret, that he locks himself in the bathroom
in the middle of the night, when his daughter's fast asleep,
so he can read volumes and volumes of dirty poetry.

June 13, 1995

The best place to turn thirty-four is in Mojácar, Spain
where the women all have fine lines on their faces
from the constant sun, which stays out long enough
to kiss the moon that fades in the day but never really goes away,
hovering just above the mountains—in Mojácar, Spain
where it is still sexy to have a tan and hips.
The houses here are all white and challenge the sun
to a boxing match of awe and brightness
so that sometimes the white turns blue from the sea
or green from the mountains or blond from the desert.
The houses are built into the sides of mountains
like teeth into gums and stand just as secure. And the hens
sing, really sing, and hold their notes better than a beginning choir.
And the sand leading to the Mediterranean is chocolate
at one end of the beach and pure sugar at the other.
And the Gypsy gives the evil eye to her client
who's gone to someone else for help because her first spell didn't work.
And there is no irony in spells or the Catholic Church,
the bells tolling from the pueblo to wake everyone up,
then reminding them at night to say their prayers.
And the women pull up their skirts, their calves in the public fountain,
and wash their clothes by hand and rub their panties and pillow cases
until the suds multiply like bubble bath, then the women carry away
jugs of water on their heads, quick and graceful as ants.
There is only the occasional satellite dish so Spaniards can laugh
at the absurdity of the O.J. Simpson trial or remark how handsome
O.J. is. Or say *Poor Nicole, we have that too you know,*
the battering of wives, in our country. In the backyard
of the house where I'm staying, the archaeologist
finds a two-thousand-year-old skull
of a small girl in what looks to be a domicile—unless, he says,
it was some kind of sacrificial altar. The dig site
is as big as a Hollywood swimming pool, full of ancient tools
and animal jaw bones. I say to someone:
Nicole Brown Simpson has been dead a year already,

she was killed last year on my birthday.
The best place to turn thirty-four is in Mojácar, Spain
where an archaeologist will cradle that girl-child's skull
in his arms for a minute before he dusts her off
and measures her eye sockets, as if he's truly sorry about what happened
all those decades and centuries and cruelties ago.

A Kissing

The *breva* is even softer than the fig—
its insides a million star-seeds that crowd the sky
or get stuck between your teeth. You can eat its skin,
which is a pale green, which to the touch
feels much like our own human skin
if it could be pulled away easily, without pain—
the soft sack of balls, the smooth wet of the vulva,
the chubby down of an earlobe. If we could turn each
other out and kiss the underside of skin
then maybe I wouldn't long for the *brevas,*
which grow only in certain short seasons
so warm flowers called *damas-de-noché*
blossom big as Chinese lanterns,
but only for one glorious night, their white
dresses lifted up above their heads. The *brevas,*
which most likely get their name from *breve*
(a Spanish word that means brief),
are often served for dessert in a bowl
made of a green cactus leaf that rocks like a breve
(an English word that means the eyelash-mark
over each short-sounding vowel
in the dictionary) that is easy to find—
but not over the word moon, which instead
is marked by a long flat horizon, a ceiling over the twin *o*s.
A kissing of the words blue and moan.

Noctilucae

They are what make the water sparkle at night—
green like neon or white like God
is floating just below the surface
with the glitter-fish. My husband and I saw them,
these noctilucae, but we didn't know what they were
as we took our after-dinner honeymoon stroll
full of flambé and coffee and shrimp
and I hiked up my dress, the hem getting sopped
by the waves anyway. They scared me, those lights
that banded together as big as our bed.
I thought: *chemical spill in the Gulf.*
I pitied the manatee, who would squint
at this brightness, as my husband walked towards
the noctilucae and tried to pick them up.
His hands came up empty, silver dust shimmering
around his calves, his loafers waiting for him
wet in the sand, the noctilucent clouds
skimming the sky like heavy cream.
It is only three years later, playing Scrabble,
challenging my husband's "nocturne,"
which I didn't know was its own word,
which I was sure was an incorrect spelling
of "nocturnal," that I find noctiluca and its plural
and think how beautiful a word. I read
what it means, realizing what we'd seen
was this—luminous flagella, the dictionary says.
I look up flagella and find the picture
of the bacteria with eyelashes but no eyes,
the bacteria too small for us to see,
the bacteria that loves the ocean and backstrokes.
My husband is sitting across from me in his sweatshirt,
picking more wooden letters from the silver pouch.
Outside is the frigid November night air
and the bald sunburned moon. I'm not upset
that I've lost my turn, that nocturne is a word—

a musical composition appropriate to the evening.
My husband didn't know what it meant either,
he confesses, he just took a chance.
The way he dove into love, the way
he reached into the summer sea trying to scoop up light.

Husband as a Second Language

You can walk a mile
if you act his age, not his shoe size.
When he does both things at once, he kills two stones.
He never counts his chickens
before his eggs or vice versa.
He doesn't care about what came first
or why certain fowls cross the road.
He throws all motion to the sinned.
He prefers to save his money for a fool
because a penny saved is a penny scorned.
He takes the bull, but never by the horns.
You only give once! Dime is of the essence!
Of course, a watch never boils,
but why should that be of surprise to anyone?
He feeds the cake, and lets them eat.
He always cooks before he leaps,
never judging a book by its brother.
He'll tell you too many books spoil the soup
so if you can't stand the beat
don't dance in the kitchen.
An old man he knew shot the bucket.
He gave a misbehaving dog a good swift lick.
Sometimes he may revise you bananas
or wake you for a ride. Even if he forgets
where he docked his car, remember:
his pen is mightier than your Ford.

The Star-Spangled Banner

I was sure then, as I sang along,
that the star-spangled banner was a glittery red gown
patterned with sequin constellations
and "Oh say" was José—
a fussy lover, the kind a woman had to dress up for,
the kind who had a small well-groomed moustache
and came from a country far away from America
where romance was even more spectacular than it was here.

José, can you see
by the dancerly light
what so proudly she hails
at the twilight's last gleaming . . .

equalled this:

José is on a balcony, his tuxedo more dapper than any other.
Or maybe he is on the deck of a cruise ship. Either way,
it's sunset and his new beloved, his own Miss America,
glides towards him in her star-spangled banner . . .
His indifference to her is unbearable. *José, can you see?*
she starts to sing. A mint toothpick dangles from his lips,
his eyes gloss over and he's in a place countries away
where all the other Josés are roasting meat over an open flame,
where señoritas huddle together in their fan-and-castanet glamour.

Who brought mites and bright stars
to the perilous fight?
All the remnants she bought
were so gallantly gleaming . . .

The red-dressed woman is used to having men notice her.
She starts to complain, whine really, interrupting José's
nostalgic dreaming. He can't stand her voice
so he clobbers his boring demanding American girlfriend

and she blinks cartoon stars, tiny flies
circling her head like planes waiting to land.
He doesn't know why he hits her exactly
except that maybe her kisses don't taste spicy enough.
He says, "You're American, I thought you were rich!"
as she fusses over a star that's fallen off her dress
and explains she made her flamenco gown herself
with material she bought on sale at a fabric store
that was going out of business in her small American town.
José's guilty hands cover his face.
He tells her he's never hit a woman before
as she pops up from the ground like a buxom Roadrunner
and shakes her coiffed head from side to side.
José reaches out his hand to help her as she lifts
her star-spangled skirt. Her legs whirl faster than fan blades
and she is off, zooming across America, leaving José
choking in the cloud of dust she trails.

José, does that star-spangled banner yet wave?

Do you miss her, José?
Do you miss the dress she sewed thinking only of you?
Did you stick around the United States
or return to a place where the women know
exactly how to please their Josés,
where your waxy facial hair will forever be in style?

She told me to tell you, José, that she forgives everything
and hopes that you're happy.
She hopes, too, that you can forgive her first-grade self
for creating you out of a song where you didn't even exist
and then having you do some pretty crummy things.
Please know that your would-be American girlfriend
still pines for you, José, somewhere in Nebraska or North Dakota.
She has a slew of kids now and her red dress is in storage.
She cries when she watches reruns of *I Love Lucy,*
Ricky's accent so much like how she remembers yours.

Playa Naturista

We're brave, but we're not *that* brave
so we go in the morning, arrive by 8:30,
when any self-respecting vacationing Spaniard
would still be in bed sleeping. I take off
my bathing-suit top first and my breasts
are surprised by the sun which they haven't seen
since they were seven or eight
when they were just nipples and seeds.
They blush pink on the empty beach
and I quickly turn over onto my stomach,
planning to stay there forever,
or at least until sundown. My husband
is in his swimming trunks, contemplating
how to get out of them—while standing up
or lying down. I look around,
suspiciously, wondering if all the other tourists
will have had implants, but it's still no one but us
and the occasional Mediterranean gull.

I close my eyes and listen to the ocean sounds—
sloshing, blood and heart, pulses,
stomach rumbles, whispering of lungs,
muscle flex, cold beer gulp, pumping,
pumping—the inside noises any body makes.

My husband nudges me and points.
The sun on the waves is a million
diamond rings. "Look," he says
as the grandma jogs by, in white sneakers
and a white visor, and nothing else.
Her breasts flop happily, her buttocks
jiggle like cove ripples. "*Hola!*"
she hollers, out of breath, all wrinkles
and sweat. She is the goddess
of nude bathing we've prayed to.

She says all bodies are beautiful
and made of water and love the sea.

My husband and I slip out of our bottoms
and run like Adam and Eve, if
Adam smoked Dunhills and Eve
wore Ray-Bans. Suddenly we're in the water
like brother and sister, like Adam and Eve
technically were. My breasts bob
like white apples, like I'm wearing a push-up bra
made of salt water. My husband
is swimming out further, at peace
with his shrinking penis which he forgets
all about because now we are dolphins
and the pleasure of water is everywhere,
swirling around each toe and pubic hair
with the same cool-womb delight.
We swim through each other's legs,
watch for fish which flash like silver
bracelets you can buy in the market.
Our fingernails are as white
as bleached bone or the stone buildings
of Mojácar. Our lips are salty and soft
and prickly as anchovies.

Our skin tightens around our bodies
as the sun moves higher in the sky.
We're having too much fun to notice.
Our watches are with our beach mats
and towels and umbrella.

When we finally look back
to the shore, we see families,
nude ones, with curly hair
and plastic pails and shovels
and Fanta Limón coolers.
We think we see a naked Jesus walk by,
the tanned hippy version
we grew up with. We see pot bellies

and stretch marks and scars.
We only hesitate a moment
before we rise out of the water, holding
each other's arms, tiptoeing on rough pebbles,
trying to keep our footing.
And we face them, all of them,
our bodies and theirs now
perfect and elegant. We are dripping
wet and full of wet tendrils,
my husband wearing only
his seaweed tie and I, a boa of kelp.